The Mediterranean Diet: Low Fat Soup, Salad, Main Dish, Breakfast and Dessert Recipes for Better Health and Natural Weight Loss

by **Alissa Noel Grey**
Text copyright(c)2016 Alissa Noel Grey

All rights reserved. No part of this publication may be reproduced, distributed, or transmitted in any form or by any means, including photocopying, recording, or other electronic or mechanical methods, without the prior written permission of the publisher, except in the case of brief quotations embodied in critical reviews and certain other noncommercial uses permitted by copyright law

Although every precaution has been taken to verify the accuracy of the information contained herein, the author and publisher assume no responsibility for any errors or omissions. No liability is assumed for damages that may result from the use of information contained within.

Table Of Contents

Healthy Mediterranean Recipes for Dinner Tonight	6
Salad and Side Dish Recipes	8
Greek Chicken Salad	9
Mediterranean Chicken and Pasta Salad	10
Vitamin Chicken Salad	11
Chicken, Lettuce and Avocado Salad	12
Mediterranean Beef Salad	13
Ground Beef Salad with Creamy Avocado Dressing	14
Tuna Salad with Lettuce and Chickpeas	16
Bean and Tuna Salad	17
Spinach, Beet and Feta Salad	18
Mediterranean Spinach Salad	19
Easy Chickpea Salad	20
Arugula and Radicchio Salad	21
Beet Salad with Walnuts	22
Warm Beet and Lentil Salad	23
Roasted Vegetable Salad	24
Mediterranean Avocado Salad	25
Granny's Favorite Couscous Salad	26
Avocado and Cucumber Salad	27
Shredded Kale and Brussels Sprout Salad	28
Homemade Hummus	29
Avocado Hummus	30
Soup Recipes	31
Moroccan Chicken Soup	32
Mediterranean Chicken Soup	34
Greek Lemon Chicken Soup	35
Bean, Chicken and Bacon Soup	36
Chicken Soup with Vermicelli	37
Italian Meatball Soup	38
Mushroom and Kale Soup	39
Creamy Brussels Sprout Soup	40
Creamy Potato Soup	41
Leek, Brown Rice and Potato Soup	42
Mediterranean Chickpea Soup	43

Creamy Tomato and Roasted Pepper Soup	44
Fast Red Lentil Soup	45
Mediterranean Lentil Soup	46
Pea, Dill and Rice Soup	47
Minted Pea and Nettle Soup	48
Bean and Pasta Soup	49
Tuscan Bean Soup	50
Italian Vegetable Soup	51
French Vegetable Soup	52
Spiced Beet and Carrot Soup	53
Main Dish Recipes	54
Chicken and Chickpea Casserole	55
Greek Chicken Casserole	56
Greek Style Chicken Skewers	57
Chicken Puttanesca	58
Meatballs with Tomato Sauce	60
Mediterranean Meatloaf with Vegetables	62
Beef Kebabs	64
Ground Beef and Brussels Sprouts	65
Hearty Meatball Stew	66
Italian Mini Meatballs	68
Marinated Beef Skewers	69
Mediterranean Steak	70
Italian Pot Roast	71
Roast Beef with Quince, Parsnips and Carrots	72
Eggplant With Ground Beef	73
Steak with Olives and Mushrooms	75
Mediterranean Beef Casserole	76
Beef with Melting Onions	77
Beef with Mushrooms	78
Beef and Spinach Stew	79
Spring Beef Stew	80
Beef Tagine with Sweet Potatoes	81
Stuffed Bell Peppers	83
Ground Beef and Cabbage Casserole	84
Ground Beef and Lentil Casserole	85

Salmon Kebabs	87
Mediterranean Baked Salmon	88
Simple Oven-Baked Sea Bass	89
Feta Cheese Baked in Foil	90
Creamy Avocado Spaghetti	91
Avocado, Roasted Mushroom and Feta Spaghetti	92
Tomato, Arugula and Feta Spaghetti	93
Mediterranean Pizza	94
Delicious One-Pot Pasta	96
Easy One-Pot Spaghetti	97
Hearty Lentil Spaghetti	98
Ratatouille	99
Spicy Chickpea and Spinach Stew	101
Moroccan Chickpea Stew	102
Zucchini Fritters	104
Baked Falafel	105
Chickpea, Rice and Mushroom Stew	106
Chickpea, Leek and Olive Stew	107
Baked Bean and Rice Casserole	108
Green Pea and Rice Casserole	109
Easy Green Bean Stew	110
Green Beans and Potatoes	111
Cabbage and Rice Stew	112
Baked Cauliflower	113
Potato and Zucchini Bake	114
Okra and Tomato Casserole	115
Breakfast and Dessert Recipes	116
Avocado and Feta Toast with Poached Eggs	117
Avocado and Olive Paste on Toasted Rye Bread	118
Avocado and Chickpea Sandwiches	119
Quick Vegetable Omelette	120
Raisin Quinoa Breakfast	121
Banana Cinnamon Fritters	122
Avocado and Pumpkin Muffins	123
Moist Pear Muffins	124
Easy Lemon Cake	125

FREE BONUS RECIPES: 20 Superfood Paleo and Vegan Smoothies for Vibrant Health and Easy Weight Loss	126
Kale and Kiwi Smoothie	127
Delicious Broccoli Smoothie	128
Papaya Smoothie	129
Beet and Papaya Smoothie	130
Lean Green Smoothie	131
Easy Antioxidant Smoothie	132
Healthy Purple Smoothie	133
Mom's Favorite Kale Smoothie	134
Creamy Green Smoothie	135
Strawberry and Arugula Smoothie	136
Emma's Amazing Smoothie	137
Good-To-Go Morning Smoothie	138
Endless Energy Smoothie	139
High-fibre Fruit Smoothie	140
Nutritious Green Smoothie	141
Apricot, Strawberry and Banana Smoothie	142
Spinach and Green Apple Smoothie	143
Superfood Blueberry Smoothie	144
Zucchini and Blueberry Smoothie	145
Tropical Spinach Smoothie	146
About the Author	147

Healthy Mediterranean Recipes for Dinner Tonight

The Mediterranean diet is not actually a "diet." Yes, it will help you lose weight and improve your health but it is really more of a relaxed and family-oriented lifestyle. It is living, cooking and eating with enthusiasm and love . People who live in the Mediterranean countries like Greece, Spain, France, Italy, Turkey and Morocco eat mainly local, everyday products that can be bought around the corner or grown in their own backyard. The Mediterranean way of cooking is in reality healthy home cooking embracing a variety of fresh ingredients such as whole grains, healthy fats, more colorful vegetables and fish, and less meat, and using wine, olive oil and fragrant herbs to create rich flavors.

Mediterranean salads are delicious, as well as diet-friendly, because they are usually served with low-carb dressings made with good fats, such as the mono-unsaturated fats found in olive oil, avocados and nuts, and lemon juice, fresh herbs and spices. Mediterranean soups and cooked meals are generally prepared slowly, all in one pot , starting with aromatic vegetables such as garlic, onions, carrots and celery gently sautéed in olive oil. Vegetable broth or water is then added, followed by herbs and spices, your choice of protein sources like fish, chicken or beans, then more vegetables, and perhaps some pasta. The ingredients which need the shortest cooking time are added last.

Unlike many diets that involve increasing your intake of certain vitamins and minerals, with the Mediterranean diet you can always improvise, invent, vary recipes, and substitute one ingredient for another. It allows you to eat a wide variety of healthy whole foods in moderation, is high in good fats and dietary fiber and extremely low in saturated fats.

The Mediterranean diet will help you:

- Eat a well-balanced diet of whole natural foods
- Prevent heart disease, diabetes, arthritis, Alzheimer's, Parkinson's and cancer

- Lower cholesterol levels and blood pressure
- Improve cardiovascular health
- Improve brain and eye health
- Eat foods that are high in good fats and dietary fiber
- Lose weight
- Increase energy

Have you ever struggled to lose weight because you couldn't stick to a "diet", or you're tired of lacking energy all the time, or simply want to get rid of all the processed foods in your diet and don't know how to go about it? If that is you - learn about the Mediterranean Diet and make a life changing shift today.

Just remember these rules to be certain that you are really following a Mediterranean diet:

- Eat vegetables with every meal and eat fresh fruit every day;
- Use olive oil when cooking. Use little or no butter at all;
- Include at least two legume meals per week – add lentils, chickpeas or beans to salads, soups or casseroles.
- Include at least two servings of fish per week: oily fish, if possible, such salmon, mackerel, gem-fish, canned sardines and canned salmon;
- Eat smaller portions of lean meat – mainly chicken, lamb, and beef;
- Eat yogurt and cheese in moderation;
- Consume wine in moderation, only with meals;
- Eat nuts, seeds, fresh fruit and dried fruit as snacks and dessert;

Salad and Side Dish Recipes

Greek Chicken Salad

Serves: 4-5

Prep time: 5 min

Ingredients:

3 chicken breast halves, cooked and sliced

1 small cucumber, sliced

2 tomatoes, sliced

1/2 red onion, sliced

1/4 cup black olives, pitted

3.5 oz feta, crumbled

2 tbsp lemon juice

2 tbsp extra virgin olive oil

1/4 cup parsley leaves, chopped

Directions:

Place the chicken, tomatoes, cucumber, red onion, olives, feta, and parsley in a salad bowl.

Toss to combine, sprinkle with lemon juice and olive oil, toss again, and serve.

Mediterranean Chicken and Pasta Salad

Serves: 5-6

Prep time: 5 min

Ingredients:

3 cups small pasta, cooked

3 chicken breast halves, cooked and shredded

1 cup cherry tomatoes, halved

1 yellow bell pepper, sliced

1 small red onion, sliced

1/2 cup black olives, pitted

2 tbsp capers

1/3 cup pine nuts, toasted

7-8 fresh basil leaves, finely chopped

for the dressing:

1/4 cup lemon juice

1/4 cup extra virgin olive oil

2 garlic cloves, crushed

salt, to taste

Directions:

Place pasta, chicken, tomatoes, bell pepper, red onion, basil, olives, capers and pine nuts in a large bowl.

Prepare the dressing by whisking lemon juice, olive oil, garlic and salt. Pour the dressing over the salad, toss to combine and serve.

Vitamin Chicken Salad

Serves: 4-5

Prep time: 5 min

Ingredients:

3 cooked chicken breasts, shredded

1 yellow bell pepper, thinly sliced

1 red bell pepper, thinly sliced

1/2 red onion, thinly sliced

1 small green apple, peeled and thinly sliced

1/2 cup toasted almonds, chopped

3 tbsp lemon juice

2 tbsp extra virgin olive oil

1 tbsp Dijon mustard

salt and pepper, to taste

Directions:

In a deep salad bowl, combine peppers, apple, chicken and almonds.

In a smaller bowl, whisk the mustard, olive oil, lemon juice, salt and pepper. Pour over the salad, toss to combine and serve.

Chicken, Lettuce and Avocado Salad

Serves: 4

Prep time: 5 min

Ingredients:

2 grilled chicken breasts, diced

1 avocado, peeled and diced

5-6 green lettuce leaves, cut in stripes

3-4 green onions, finely chopped

5-6 radishes, sliced

7-8 grape tomatoes, halved

3 tbsp lemon juice

3 tbsp extra virgin olive oil

1 tsp dried mint

salt and black pepper, to taste

Directions:

In a deep salad bowl, combine avocados, lettuce, chicken, onions, radishes and grape tomatoes.

Season with dried mint, salt and pepper to taste. Sprinkle with lemon juice and olive oil, toss lightly, and serve.

Mediterranean Beef Salad

Serves: 4-5

Prep time: 5 min

Ingredients:

8 oz quality roast beef, thinly sliced

1 avocado, peeled and diced

2 tomatoes, diced

1 cucumber, peeled and diced

1 yellow pepper, sliced

2 carrots, shredded

1 cup black olives, pitted and halved

2-3 fresh basil leaves, torn

2-3 fresh oregano leaves

1 tbsp balsamic vinegar

4 tbsp extra virgin olive oil

salt and black pepper, to taste

Directions:

Combine the avocado and all vegetables in a large salad bowl. Add in basil and oregano leaves.

Season with salt and pepper, drizzle with balsamic vinegar and olive oil, and toss to combine. Top with roast beef and serve.

Ground Beef Salad with Creamy Avocado Dressing

Serves: 4-5

Prep time: 5 min

Ingredients:

1 green lettuce, cut in stripes

2-3 green onions, finely cut

1 garlic clove, crushed

½ cup black olives, pitted and halved

4-5 radishes, sliced

8 oz ground beef

2 tbsp extra virgin olive oil

1/2 tsp ground cumin

1/2 tsp dried oregano

1 tsp paprika

salt and pepper, to taste

for the dressing:

1 avocado, peeled and cut

1 tbsp extra virgin olive oil

4 tbsp lemon juice

2 garlic cloves, cut

1 tbsp water

Directions:

Blend the dressing ingredients until smooth.

Heat olive oil in a medium saucepan and gently cook the ground beef and the seasonings, stirring, for 5-6 minutes, or until cooked through.

Place lettuce, cooked beef and all other salad ingredients in a bowl. Toss well to combine. Drizzle with dressing and serve.

Tuna Salad with Lettuce and Chickpeas

Serves: 4

Prep time: 5 min

Ingredients:

1 head green lettuce, washed cut in thin strips

1 cup chopped watercress

1 cucumber, peeled and chopped

1 tomato, diced

1 can tuna, drained and broken into small chunks

1/2 cup chickpeas, from a can

7-8 radishes, sliced

3-4 spring onions, chopped

juice of half lemon

3 tbsp extra virgin olive oil

Directions:

Mix all the vegetables in a large bowl. Add the tuna and the chickpeas and season with lemon juice, oil and salt to taste.

Bean and Tuna Salad

Serves: 4

Prep time: 5 min

Ingredients:

1 can white beans, rinsed and drained

1 cup cooked tuna, broken into chunks

1/2 red onion, chopped

juice of one lemon

1/2 cup fresh parsley leaves, chopped

1 tsp dried mint

salt and black pepper, to taste

3 tbsp extra virgin olive oil

Directions:

Put tuna chunks and beans in a salad bowl and toss to combine. Add in onions, parsley, mint, lemon juice and olive oil, and toss to combine.

Season with salt and black pepper to taste. Serve chilled.

Spinach, Beet and Feta Salad

Serves: 4-5

Prep time: 15 min

Ingredients:

3 medium beets, steamed, peeled and diced

1 bag baby spinach leaves

1/2 cup walnuts, toasted

4 oz feta, crumbled

4-5 spring onions, chopped

for the dressing:

1 garlic clove, crushed

2 tbsp extra virgin olive oil

2 tbsp lemon juice

1 tbsp finely chopped dill

Directions:

Wash the beets well, steam, peel and dice them. Arrange the spinach leaves in a large salad bowl. Scatter the beets, onions, walnuts and feta over the spinach.

In a smaller bowl or cup, combine the oil, lemon juice, garlic and dill. Whisk until smooth, season with salt and pepper, and drizzle over the salad.

Mediterranean Spinach Salad

Serves: 4

Prep time: 15 min

Ingredients:

1 bag baby spinach

4-5 spring onions, finely chopped

1 cucumber, peeled and cut

1/2 cup walnuts, halved and roasted

1/3 cup yogurt

2 tbsp red wine vinegar

3 tbsp extra virgin olive oil

salt and black pepper, to taste

Directions:

Whisk yogurt, olive oil and vinegar in a small bowl. Place the baby spinach leaves in a large salad bowl.

Add the onions, cucumber and walnuts. Season with black pepper and salt, stir, and toss with the dressing.

Easy Chickpea Salad

Serves: 3-4

Prep time: 2-3 min

Ingredients:

1 15 oz can chickpeas, drained

1 medium red onion, finely cut

1 cucumber, peeled and diced

2 tomatoes, sliced

a bunch of radishes, sliced

½ cup fresh parsley, finely chopped

2 tbsp extra virgin olive oil

1 tbsp balsamic vinegar

salt, to taste

4 oz crumbled feta cheese, to serve

Directions:

In a salad bowl, toss together the chickpeas, onion, cucumber, tomatoes, radishes and parsley.

Add in the balsamic vinegar, olive oil and salt and stir. Serve sprinkled with crumbled feta cheese.

Arugula and Radicchio Salad

Serves: 4

Prep time: 5 min

Ingredients:

1 bunch arugula leaves

1 small head radicchio, chopped

1 avocado, peeled and cubed

1/2 cup pomegranate seeds, from 1 medium pomegranate

1/3 cup hazelnuts

for the dressing:

1 tbsp honey

1 tbsp balsamic vinegar

2 tbsp extra virgin olive oil

1/2 tsp salt

Directions:

Place arugula, radicchio, avocado, hazelnuts and pomegranate seeds in a large salad bowl and gently toss to combine.

Whisk dressing ingredients until smooth, pour over the salad, serve and enjoy!

Beet Salad with Walnuts

Serves: 4

Prep time: 25 min

Ingredients:

3 medium beets, steamed and diced

1 red onion, sliced

1/2 cup walnuts, halved

1 cup strained yogurt

1 tbsp lemon juice

2 tbsp olive oil

4-5 mint leaves, chopped

½ tsp salt

Directions:

Wash the beets, trim the stems, and steam them over boiling water until cooked through.

Dice the beets and place them in a salad bowl. Add in walnuts and onion and toss to combine. Sprinkle with fresh mint leaves.

Whisk the yogurt with garlic, olive oil and lemon juice until smooth. Pour over the diced beets and toss to combine. Serve cold.

Warm Beet and Lentil Salad

Serves: 5-6

Prep time: 10 min

Ingredients:

1 14 oz can brown lentils, drained, rinsed

1 14 oz can sliced pickled beets, drained

1 cup baby arugula leaves

1 small red onion, chopped

2 garlic cloves, crushed

6 oz feta cheese, crumbled

1 tbsp extra virgin olive oil

for the dressing

3 tbsp extra virgin olive oil

1 tbsp red wine vinegar

1 tsp summer savory

salt and black pepper, to taste

Directions:

Heat one tablespoon of olive oil in a frying pan and gently sauté onion for 2-3 minutes or until softened. Add in garlic, lentils and beets. Cook, stirring, for 2 minutes.

Whisk together remaining olive oil, vinegar, summer savory, salt and pepper. Add to the lentils and toss to coat. Combine baby arugula, feta and lentil mixture in a bowl. Toss gently to combine and serve.

Roasted Vegetable Salad

Serves: 4-5

Prep time: 30 min

Ingredients:

3 tomatoes, halved

1 zucchini, quartered

1 fennel bulb, thinly sliced

2 small eggplants, ends trimmed, quartered

1 large red pepper, halved, deseeded, cut into strips

2 medium onions, quartered

1 tsp oregano

2 tbsp extra virgin olive oil

for the dressing

2/3 cup yogurt

1 tbsp fresh lemon juice

1 small garlic clove, chopped

Directions:

Place the zucchini, eggplant, pepper, fennel, onions, tomatoes and olive oil on a lined baking sheet. Season with salt, pepper and oregano and roast in a 500 degrees F oven until golden, about 20 minutes.

Whisk the yogurt, lemon juice and garlic in a bowl. Taste and season with salt and pepper. Divide the vegetables in 4-5 plates. Top with the yogurt mixture and serve.

Mediterranean Avocado Salad

Serves: 5-6

Prep time: 10 min

Ingredients:

2 avocados, peeled, halved and cut into cubes

½ ciabatta roll, cut into small cubes

2 cups cherry tomatoes, halved

½ red onion, thinly sliced

1 large cucumber, halved, sliced

½ cup green olives, pitted, halved

½ cup black olives, pitted, sliced

6 oz feta cheese, cut into cubes

7-8 fresh basil leaves, torn

½ cup parsley leaves, finely cut

4 tbsp extra virgin olive oil

3 tbsp red wine vinegar

Directions:

Line a baking tray with baking paper and place ciabatta cubes. Drizzle with one tablespoon of olive oil. Season with salt and pepper and gently toss to coat. Cook under the grill for 2-3 minutes or until golden. Set aside to cool.

Place all vegetables, feta, basil, olives, and ciabatta cubes in a large salad bowl. Gently toss to combine then sprinkle with vinegar and remaining olive oil.

Season with salt and pepper and gently toss again. Sprinkle with parsley and serve.

Granny's Favorite Couscous Salad

Serves: 4

Prep time: 15 min

Ingredients:

1 cup medium couscous

1 1/2 cup hot water

3 ripe tomatoes, diced

1/2 cup black olives, pitted and chopped

5 green onions, finely chopped

4 tbsp extra virgin olive oil

4 tbsp lemon juice

1 tbsp dry mint

2-3 fresh mint leaves

salt, to taste

Directions:

Place the couscous in a large bowl and pour over a cup and a half of boiling water. Stir, cover, and set aside for 10 minutes. Fluff with a fork and stir in the tomatoes, olives and onions.

In a small bowl, whisk olive oil, lemon juice, dried mint, fresh mint and salt. Pour over the couscous salad, stir until well combined and serve.

Avocado and Cucumber Salad

Serves: 4-5

Prep time: 5 min

Ingredients:

2 avocados, peeled, halved and sliced

½ red onion, thinly sliced

1 large cucumber, halved, sliced

½ radicchio, trimmed, finely shredded

7-8 fresh basil leaves, torn

for the dressing:

1 tbsp black olive paste

2 tbsp extra virgin olive oil

1 tbsp red balsamic vinegar

1 tbsp lemon juice

salt and pepper, to taste

Directions:

Combine avocado, radicchio and cucumber in a bowl.

Place vinegar, oil, lemon juice and black olive paste in a small bowl and whisk until very well combined.

Pour over the salad, season with salt and pepper and toss gently to combine.

Shredded Kale and Brussels Sprout Salad

Serves: 4-6

Prep time: 5 min

Ingredients:

18-29 Brussels sprouts, shredded

1 cup finely shredded kale

1/2 cup grated Parmesan or Pecorino cheese

1 cup walnuts, halved, toasted

1/2 cup dried cranberries

for the dressing:

6 tbsp extra virgin olive oil

2 tbsp apple cinder vinegar

1 tbsp Dijon mustard

salt and pepper, to taste

Directions:

Shred the Brussels sprouts and kale in a food processor or mandolin. Toss them in a bowl, top with toasted walnuts, cranberries and grated cheese.

In a smaller bowl, whisk the olive oil, apple cider vinegar and mustard until smooth. Pour the dressing over the salad, stir and serve.

Homemade Hummus

Serves: 5-6

Prep time: 5 min

Ingredients:

1 15 oz can chickpeas, drained

1/3 cup tahini paste

3 tbsp extra virgin olive oil

½ lemon, juiced

2-3 small garlic cloves, chopped

1-2 tsp cumin, or to taste

1 tsp salt

water from the chickpea can

extra virgin olive oil, parsley, paprika for serving

Directions:

Drain the chickpeas and keep the juice in a small cup. If possible, remove the skins from the chickpeas. Place the chickpeas in the blender and pulse.

Add the tahini, lemon juice, garlic, olive oil, cumin and salt, and blend until smooth, gradually adding the chickpea water to the mix until the mixture is completely smooth.

To serve, top with olive oil, parsley, and sprinkle with paprika.

Avocado Hummus

Serves: 4

Prep time: 2-3 min

Ingredients:

1 15 oz can chickpeas, drained

1 medium avocado, chopped

2 tbsp tahini

1/4 cup lemon juice

1 garlic clove, crushed

2 tbsp finely cut parsley

1 tbsp extra virgin olive oil

½ tsp paprika

a pinch of cumin

Directions:

Heat oil in a small frying pan over medium-high heat. Add half the chickpeas and cook, stirring, for 3-4 minutes or until just golden. Remove from heat and set aside to cool.

Blend remaining chickpeas with avocado, tahini, lemon juice, garlic and cumin until smooth. Season with salt and pepper, to taste, and spoon the avocado hummus into a serving bowl.

Top with chickpeas and sprinkle with paprika and parsley.

Soup Recipes

Moroccan Chicken Soup

Serves: 5-6

Prep time: 30 min

Ingredients:

3-4 skinless, boneless chicken thighs, cut into bite-sized pieces

1 onion, finely cut

2 garlic cloves, chopped

1 small zucchini, diced

2 cups butternut squash, peeled and cut in 1/2-inch pieces

2 tbsp tomato paste

4 cups chicken broth

1/3 cup uncooked couscous

1/2 tsp ground cumin

1/4 teaspoon ground cinnamon

1 tbsp paprika

1 tbsp dried basil

2 tbsp orange zest

3 tbsp extra virgin olive oil

Directions:

Heat olive oil in a soup pot over medium heat. Gently sauté onion, for 1 minute, stirring. Add in garlic, basil and chicken, and cook for 2-3 minutes, or until chicken is sealed.

Stir in cumin, cinnamon and paprika. Add butternut squash and stir. Dissolve the tomato paste in the chicken broth and add to the soup.

Bring to a boil, reduce heat and simmer for 10-15 minutes.

Stir in couscous, salt, and zucchini and cook until the butternut squash is tender.

Remove from heat, season with salt and pepper to taste, stir in orange rind, and serve.

Mediterranean Chicken Soup

Serves: 6-8

Prep time: 35 min

Ingredients:

3 chicken breast halves

2 carrots, chopped

1 celery stalk, chopped

1 small onion, chopped

1/3 cup rice

8 cups water

1/2 cup olives, pitted and halved

salt and black pepper, to taste

1/2 cup fresh coriander, finely cut, to serve

lemon juice, to serve

Directions:

Place chicken breasts in a soup pot together with onion, carrots, celery, salt, black pepper, and water.

Bring to a boil, add in rice and olives, stir, and reduce heat. Simmer for 30-35 minutes then remove the chicken from the pot and let it cool slightly.

Shred the chicken and return it back to the pot. Stir, and serve sprinkled with fresh coriander and lemon juice.

Greek Lemon Chicken Soup

Serves: 4

Prep time: 35 min

Ingredients:

3 chicken breast halves, diced

1/3 cup rice

4 cups chicken broth

1 small onion, finely cut

3 raw egg yolks

1/2 cup fresh lemon juice

3 tbsp extra virgin olive oil

1 tsp salt

1/2 tsp black pepper

1/2 cup fresh parsley, finely cut, to serve

Directions:

In a soup pot, heat the olive oil and gently sauté the onion until translucent. Add in the chicken broth and bring to a boil.

Stir in the rice and the chicken, reduce heat, and simmer until the rice is almost done.

Whisk the egg yolks and lemon juice together in a small bowl. Gently add in a cup of the broth whisking constantly.

Return this mixture to the chicken soup and stir well to blend. Do not boil any more. Season with salt and pepper, and garnish with finely chopped parsley. Serve hot.

Bean, Chicken and Bacon Soup

Serves 4-5

Prep time: 35 min

Ingredients:

2-3 bacon strips, cut

2 cups cooked and diced chicken

1/2 can kidney beans, rinsed and drained

1 small onion, chopped

2 garlic cloves, chopped

3 cups water

1/2 can tomatoes, diced, undrained

1 bay leaf

1/2 tsp dried oregano

1/2 tsp dried basil

salt and pepper, to taste

Directions:

In a deep soup pot, gently cook onion and bacon, stirring, for 3-4 minutes. Add in the garlic and cook until just fragrant.

Add in water, tomatoes and seasonings and bring to a boil. Cover, reduce heat and simmer for 30 minutes. Add in chicken and beans. Simmer for five minutes more and serve.

Chicken Soup with Vermicelli

Serves 4

Prep time: 40 min

Ingredients:

3 chicken breast halves

1/2 onion, finely cut

1 garlic clove, chopped

1/2 cup vermicelli

1 carrot, grated

4 cups water

1 tsp salt

1/2 tsp black pepper

1 egg, beaten

2 tbsp lemon juice

Directions:

Place the chicken breasts and the onion in a soup pot together with 4 cups of water. Add in 1 tsp salt and bring to a boil.

Cook for 30 minutes or until the chicken is cooked through then take it out of the pot, let it cool a little, dice it, and put it back in the soup.

Stir in carrot, garlic and vermicelli. Reduce heat and simmer over medium heat for 5 minutes.

Whisk the egg and lemon juice in a bowl and slowly stir this mixture into the soup. Do not boil it again.

Italian Meatball Soup

Serves 4-5

Prep time: 30 min

Ingredients:

1 lb ground beef

1 small onion, grated

1 onion, chopped

1 egg, lightly beaten

2 garlic cloves, crushed

1 cup baby spinach, coarsely chopped

4-5 fresh basil leaves, finely chopped

1 cup tomato sauce

3 cups beef broth

2 tbsp extra virgin olive oil

salt and black pepper, to taste

Directions:

Combine ground beef, onion, garlic, and egg in a large bowl. Season with salt and pepper to taste. Mix well with hands and roll teaspoonfuls of the mixture into balls. Place meatballs on a large plate.

Heat olive oil into a large deep saucepan and sauté onion and garlic until transparent. Add in tomato sauce and broth and bring to a boil over high heat. Stir in meatballs. Reduce heat to medium-low and simmer, uncovered, for 20 minutes.

Add in spinach, basil, salt, and pepper and simmer, uncovered, until spinach is wilted, about 1 minute.

Mushroom and Kale Soup

Serves: 4-5

Prep time: 30 min

Ingredients:

1 onion, chopped

1 carrot, chopped

1 zucchini, peeled and diced

1 potato, peeled and diced

10 white mushrooms, chopped

1 bunch kale (10 oz), stemmed and coarsely chopped

3 cups vegetable broth

4 tbsp extra virgin olive oil

salt and black pepper, to taste

Directions:

Gently heat olive oil in a large soup pot. Add in onions, carrot and mushrooms and cook until vegetables are tender. Stir in zucchini, kale and vegetable broth.

Season to taste with salt and pepper and simmer for 20 minutes.

Creamy Brussels Sprout Soup

Serves: 4-5

Prep time: 30 min

Ingredients:

1 lb frozen Brussels sprouts, thawed

2 potatoes, peeled and chopped

1 large onion, chopped

3 garlic cloves, minced

4 cups vegetable broth

3 tbsp extra virgin olive oil

1/2 tsp curry powder

salt and black pepper, to taste

Directions:

Gently heat olive oil in a large saucepan over medium-high heat. Cook onion and garlic and for 3-4 minutes until tender. Add in Brussels sprouts, potato, curry and vegetable broth.

Cover and bring to a boil, then reduce heat and simmer for 20 minutes, stirring from time to time. Remove from heat and blend until smooth. Return to pan and cook until heated through.

Creamy Potato Soup

Serves: 4-5

Prep time: 35 min

Ingredients:

6 medium potatoes, cut into small cubes

1 leek, white part only, chopped

1 carrot, chopped

1 zucchini, peeled and chopped

1 celery stalk, chopped

3 cups water

1 cup milk

3 tbsp extra virgin olive oil

salt and black pepper, to taste

Directions:

Gently heat olive oil in a deep saucepan and sauté the onion for 2-3 minutes. Add in potatoes, carrot, zucchini and celery and cook for 2-3 minutes, stirring.

Add in water and salt and bring to a boil, then lower heat and simmer until the vegetables are tender. Blend until smooth, add milk, blend some more and serve.

Leek, Brown Rice and Potato Soup

Serves: 4-5

Prep time: 35 min

Ingredients:

3 potatoes, peeled and diced

2 leeks, finely chopped

1/4 cup brown rice

5 cups water

3 tbsp extra virgin olive oil

lemon juice, to taste

Directions:

Heat olive oil in a deep soup pot and sauté leeks for 3-4 minutes. Add in potatoes and cook for a minute more.

Stir in water, bring to a boil, and the brown rice. Reduce heat and simmer for 30 minutes.

Add lemon juice, to taste, and serve.

Mediterranean Chickpea Soup

Serves: 5-6

Prep time: 30 min

Ingredients:

1 can (15 oz) chickpeas, drained

1 small onion, chopped

2 garlic cloves, minced

1 can (15 oz) tomatoes, diced

2 cups vegetable broth

1 cup milk

3 tbsp extra virgin olive oil

2 bay leaves

1/2 tsp dried oregano

Directions:

Heat olive oil in a deep soup pot and sauté onion and garlic for 1-2 minutes. Add in broth, chickpeas, tomatoes, bay leaves, and oregano.

Bring the soup to a boil then reduce heat and simmer for 20 minutes. Add in milk and cook for 1-2 minutes more.

Set aside to cool, discard the bay leaves and blend until smooth.

Creamy Tomato and Roasted Pepper Soup

Serves: 4-5

Prep time: 35 min

Ingredients:

1 (12-ounce) jar roasted red peppers, drained and chopped

1 large onion, chopped

2 garlic cloves, minced

4 medium tomatoes, chopped

4 cups vegetable broth

3 tbsp extra virgin olive oil

2 bay leaves

Directions:

Heat olive oil in a large saucepan over medium-high heat and sauté onion for 3-4 minutes, stirring. Add in garlic and sauté until just fragrant.

Stir in the red peppers, bay leaves and tomatoes and simmer for 10 minutes. Add broth, season with salt and pepper, and bring to the boil.

Reduce heat and simmer for 20 minutes. Set aside to cool slightly, remove the bay leaves and blend, in batches, until smooth.

Fast Red Lentil Soup

Serves: 4-5

Prep time: 20 min

Ingredients:

1 cup red lentils

1/2 small onion, chopped

2 garlic cloves, chopped

1/2 red pepper, chopped

3 cups vegetable broth

1 cup coconut milk

3 tbsp extra virgin olive oil

1 tbsp paprika

1/2 tsp ginger

1 tsp cumin

salt and black pepper, to taste

Directions:

Gently heat olive oil in a large saucepan. Add onion, garlic, red pepper, paprika, ginger and cumin and sauté, stirring, until just fragrant. Add in red lentils and vegetable broth.

Bring to a boil, cover, and simmer for 20 minutes. Add in coconut milk and simmer for 5 more minutes.

Remove from heat, season with salt and black pepper, and blend until smooth. Serve hot.

Mediterranean Lentil Soup

Serves: 4-5

Prep time: 35 min

Ingredients:

1 cup red lentils

2 carrots, chopped

1 onion, chopped

1 garlic clove, chopped

1 small red pepper, chopped

1 can tomatoes, chopped

½ can chickpeas, drained

½ can white beans, drained

1 small celery stalk, chopped

6 cups water

1 tbsp paprika

1 tsp ginger, grated

1 tsp cumin

3 tbsp extra virgin olive oil

Directions:

Heat olive oil in a deep soup pot and gently sauté onions, garlic, red pepper and ginger. Add in water, lentils, chickpeas, white beans, tomatoes, carrots, celery, and cumin.

Bring to a boil then lower heat and simmer for 35 minutes, or until the lentils are tender. Purée half the soup in a food processor. Return the puréed soup to the pot, stir and serve.

Pea, Dill and Rice Soup

Serves: 4

Prep time: 25 min

Ingredients:

1 (16 oz) bag frozen green peas

1 onion, chopped

3-4 garlic cloves, chopped

1/3 cup rice

3 tbsp fresh dill, chopped

3 tbsp extra virgin olive oil

fresh dill, finely chopped, to serve

salt and pepper, to taste

Directions:

Heat oil in a large saucepan over medium-high heat and sauté onion and garlic for 3-4 minutes.

Add in peas and vegetable broth and bring to the boil. Stir in rice, cover, reduce heat, and simmer for 15 minutes. Add dill, season with salt and pepper and serve sprinkled with fresh dill.

Minted Pea and Nettle Soup

Serves: 4

Prep time: 25 min

Ingredients:

1 onion, chopped

3-4 garlic cloves, chopped

4 cups vegetable broth

2 tbsp dried mint leaves

1 16 oz bag frozen green peas

about 20 nettle tops

3 tbsp extra virgin olive oil

fresh dill, finely chopped, to serve

Directions:

Heat oil in a large saucepan over medium-high heat and sauté onion and garlic for 3-4 minutes.

Add in dried mint, peas, washed nettles, and vegetable broth and bring to the boil. Cover, reduce heat, and simmer for 10 minutes. Remove from heat and set aside to cool slightly, then blend in batches, until smooth.

Return soup to saucepan over medium-low heat and cook until heated through. Season with salt and pepper. Serve sprinkled with fresh dill.

Bean and Pasta Soup

Serves: 4-5

Prep time: 10-15 min

Ingredients:

1 onion, chopped

2 large carrots, chopped

2 garlic cloves, minced

1 cup cooked orzo

1 15 oz can white beans, rinsed and drained

1 15 oz can tomatoes, diced and undrained

1 cup baby spinach leaves

3 cups vegetable broth

1 tbsp paprika

1 tbsp dried mint

3 tbsp extra virgin olive oil

salt and black pepper, to taste

Directions:

Heat the olive oil over medium heat and gently sauté the onion, garlic and carrots. Add in tomatoes, broth, salt and pepper, and bring to a boil.

Reduce heat and cook for 5-10 minutes, or until the carrots are tender. Stir in orzo, beans and spinach, and simmer until spinach is wilted.

Tuscan Bean Soup

Serves: 4-5

Prep time: 10-15 min

Ingredients:

1 onion, chopped

1 large carrot, chopped

2 garlic cloves, minced

1 15 oz can white beans, rinsed and drained

1 cup spinach leaves, trimmed and washed

3 cups vegetable broth

1 tbsp paprika

1 tbsp dried mint

3 tbsp extra virgin olive oil

salt and black pepper, to taste

Directions:

Heat the olive oil over medium heat and gently sauté the onion, garlic and carrot. Add in beans, broth, salt and pepper and bring to a boil.

Reduce heat and cook for 10 minutes, or until the carrots are tender. Stir in spinach, and simmer for about 5 minutes, until spinach is wilted.

Italian Vegetable Soup

Serves: 4-5

Prep time: 25 min

Ingredients:

1/2 onion, chopped

2 garlic cloves, chopped

¼ cabbage, chopped

1 carrot, chopped

2 celery stalks, chopped

3 cups water

1 cup canned tomatoes, diced, undrained

1 1/2 cup green beans, trimmed and cut into 1/2-inch pieces

1/2 cup pasta, cooked

2-3 fresh basil leaves

2 tbsp extra virgin olive oil

black pepper and salt, to taste

Directions:

Heat the olive oil in a large pot over medium-high heat. Add the onion and cook until translucent, about 4 minutes. Add in the garlic, carrot and celery and cook for 5 minutes more.

Stir in the green beans, cabbage, tomatoes, basil, and water and bring to a boil. Reduce heat and simmer uncovered, for 15 minutes, or until vegetables are tender.

Stir in pasta, season with pepper and salt to taste and serve.

French Vegetable Soup

Serves: 4-5

Prep time: 25 min

Ingredients:

2 leeks, white and pale green parts only, well rinsed and thinly sliced

1 large zucchini, peeled and diced

1 medium fennel bulb, trimmed, cored, and cut into large chunks

2 garlic cloves, chopped

3 cups vegetable broth

1 cup canned tomatoes, drained and chopped

1/2 cup vermicelli, broken into small pieces

3 tbsp extra virgin olive oil

black pepper, to taste

Directions:

Heat the olive oil in a large stockpot. Add the leeks and sauté over low heat for 5 minutes. Add in the zucchini, fennel and garlic and cook for about 5 minutes.

Stir in the vegetable broth and the tomatoes and bring to the boil. Reduce heat and simmer, uncovered, for 20 minutes, or until the vegetables are tender but still holding their shape.

Stir in the vermicelli. Simmer for a further 5 minutes and serve.

Spiced Beet and Carrot Soup

Serves: 4-5

Prep time: 25 min

Ingredients:

3 beets, washed and peeled

2 carrots, peeled and chopped

1 small onion, chopped

1 garlic clove, chopped

3 cups vegetable broth

1 cup water

2 tbsp extra virgin olive oil

1 tsp grated ginger

1 tsp grated orange peel

Directions:

Heat the olive oil in a large stockpot. Add the onion and sauté over low heat for 3-4 minutes or until translucent. Add the garlic, beets, carrots, ginger and lemon rind.

Stir in water and vegetable broth and bring to the boil. Reduce heat to medium and simmer, partially covered, for 30 minutes, or until beets are tender.

Cool slightly and blend soup in batches until smooth. Season with salt and pepper and serve.

Main Dish Recipes

Chicken and Chickpea Casserole

Serves: 4

Prep time: 40 min

Ingredients:

8 chicken drumsticks

2 leeks, trimmed, thinly sliced

1 garlic clove, crushed

1 can chickpeas, drained and rinsed

1 can tomatoes

1 tsp dried rosemary

3 tbsp extra virgin olive oil

cooked couscous, to serve

Directions:

In a casserole, gently heat the oil over medium-high heat. Brown the chicken tights for 1-2 minutes, each side.

Add in leeks and garlic and cook, stirring, for 2 minutes or until soft. Add in tomatoes, chickpeas, and rosemary and bring to a boil.

Cover and simmer for 35 minutes or until the chicken is tender. Season with salt and pepper and serve with couscous.

Greek Chicken Casserole

Serves: 4

Prep time: 45 min

Ingredients:

8 chicken tights

1 onion, chopped

4-5 potatoes, cubed

1 carrot, chopped

1 lb green beans, trimmed and chopped

1 cup diced, tomatoes

2 garlic cloves, chopped

1 cup feta cheese, crumbled

3 tbsp extra virgin olive oil

salt and black pepper, to taste

Directions:

Heat oil in a large casserole dish over medium heat. Add in onion and chicken and cook for a minute, stirring. Add in black pepper, carrot and garlic and sauté for another minute.

Add in potatoes and cook for 2 minutes, or until they begin to brown. Stir in beans and tomatoes.

Sprinkle with salt and black pepper to taste and top with feta. Cover, and bake for 40 minutes, stirring halfway through.

Greek Style Chicken Skewers

Serves: 4

Prep time: 50 min

Ingredients:

2 lbs chicken breasts, diced

3 small zucchinis, diced

12 white button mushrooms

3 tbsp extra virgin olive oil

1 lemon, juiced

2 garlic cloves, crushed

1 tsp dried oregano

1 tsp dried rosemary

12 wooden skewers

Directions:

Thread chicken, mushrooms and zucchinis alternately onto each of 12 skewers. Place in a shallow dish. Combine extra virgin olive oil and lemon juice, garlic and oregano.

Pour over chicken. Turn to coat. Marinate for at least 30 minutes.

Preheat a barbecue plate on medium-high heat. Cook skewers for 4 minutes each side or until chicken is just cooked through.

Chicken Puttanesca

Serves: 4

Prep time: 30 min

Ingredients:

4 boneless chicken breasts

2 tbsp extra virgin olive oil

for the sauce:

2 tbsp extra virgin olive oil

4 garlic cloves, crushed

1 small onion, diced

1/2 cup green olives, pitted and chopped

2 tbsp capers, drained and coarsely chopped

3 boneless anchovy fillets, coarsely chopped

2 tomatoes, diced

1 tbsp tomato paste

1 tbsp paprika

salt and black pepper, to taste

Directions:

Heat two tablespoons of olive oil in a large skillet and brown the chicken for about 2 minutes, each side. Cover with a lid and cook for about 10-15 minutes, or until cooked through. Set aside on 4 plates.

In the same skillet, heat two tablespoons of olive oil. Add in garlic, onions, anchovies, olives, capers and paprika. Gently sauté these ingredients, stirring constantly, for about one minute.

Add in the tomatoes and tomato paste, season with salt and pepper and cook over high heat for 5-6 minutes or until the tomatoes are cooked and the sauce thickens.

Divide the sauce between the chicken breasts and serve.

Meatballs with Tomato Sauce

Serves: 4-5

Prep time: 30 min

Ingredients:

2 lbs ground beef

1 onion, very finely cut

2 eggs, lightly whisked

1 tbsp chia seeds

1 tbsp parsley, finely chopped

1/2 tsp cumin

1/2 tsp ground ginger

2 tbsp extra virgin olive oil

1 can tomatoes diced tomatoes, undrained

1 tbsp tomato paste

1 cup chicken broth

Directions:

Preheat the oven to 350 F. Line a baking tray with baking paper.

Combine the ground beef, onion, eggs, chia seeds, parsley, salt and cumin in a bowl. Using your hands, mix everything until it well combined. Roll beef mixture into walnut sized meatballs and arrange them on the baking tray. Bake for 10 minutes until light golden.

In a deep saucepan, heat olive oil over medium heat. Stir in ginger, tomatoes and tomato paste. Add chicken broth and bring to a boil, then reduce heat and simmer for 5 minutes. Add the meatballs and simmer for 20 more minutes or until the meat is cooked through and the sauce has thickened.

Mediterranean Meatloaf with Vegetables

Serves: 4-5

Prep time: 45 min

Ingredients:

2 lbs ground beef

2 eggs, lightly beaten

1/3 cup almond meal

1 zucchini, peeled and diced

2 small tomatoes, halved

5-6 white mushrooms, halved

2 small onions, peeled and quartered

2-3 small parsnips

1/3 cup chicken broth

4 tbsp extra virgin olive oil

1 cup fresh parsley, finely cut

1 tsp dried oregano

1 tsp garlic powder

1/2 tsp black pepper

Directions:

Place ground beef, eggs, almond meal, parsley, salt, garlic powder and black pepper in a bowl and combine well with hands. Prepare a loaf and place it in the center of a baking dish.

Arrange vegetables around the meatloaf, add in chicken broth, sprinkle with dried oregano and season with salt to taste. Bake in a preheated to 350 F oven for 40 minutes.

Beef Kebabs

Serves: 4

Prep time: 20 min

Ingredients:

2 lb ground beef

1 onion, cut

1 tbsp tomato paste

1 tsp cumin

1 tbsp dried parsley

1 tsp dried mint

1/2 tsp black pepper

1/2 tsp sumac

bamboo skewers

Directions:

In a food processor, place onion, parsley, mint, black pepper and sumac. Process until finely chopped.

Combine ground beef with the onion mixture and mix well with hands. Roll tablespoonfuls of the meat mixture into balls. Thread 3-4 meatballs onto 1 skewer.

Preheat BBQ grill to medium heat. Grill the kebabs for about 2-3 minutes each side for medium cooked.

Ground Beef and Brussels Sprouts

Serves: 4

Prep time: 20 min

Ingredients:

6 oz ground beef

1/2 onion, finely cut

2 garlic cloves, crushed

½ cup grated sweet potato

1 cup grated Brussels sprouts

1 egg, boiled

1 tbsp extra virgin olive oil

Directions:

In a medium saucepan, heat the olive oil over medium heat. Gently sauté the onion and garlic until the onion is soft and translucent. Add in the beef and the sweet potato and cook until the meat is fully cooked.

Stir in the Brussels sprouts and cook for about 5 minutes more. Season with salt and pepper to taste and serve topped with a boiled egg.

Hearty Meatball Stew

Serves: 6

Prep time: 35 min

Ingredients:

for the meatballs:

2 lbs ground beef

1 onion, finely copped

1/3 cup parsley leaves, finely chopped

for the sauce:

1/2 small onion, chopped

1 carrot, chopped

1 red pepper, cut

1 zucchini, peeled and cut

1/2 eggplant, peeled and diced

2 garlic cloves, chopped

4 white mushrooms, sliced

1 can tomatoes, diced, undrained

1/2 cup chicken broth

tbsp extra virgin olive oil

1/2 cup parsley leaves, to serve

salt and black pepper, to taste

Directions:

Combine ground beef, onion, parsley, salt and pepper in a bowl.

Roll tablespoonfuls of beef mixture into balls and set aside on plate.

Heat olive oil in a deep frying pan. Gently sauté the onion, pepper, carrot and garlic for 2-3 minutes, stirring. Add in the mushrooms, eggplant and zucchini, stir and cook for 2-3 minutes more. Add in tomatoes and chicken broth and bring to a boil over medium heat.

Drop beef meatballs into tomato mixture. Reduce heat to low and simmer, uncovered, for 30 minutes or until the meatballs are cooked through. Sprinkle with parsley and serve.

Italian Mini Meatballs

Serves: 6

Prep time: 35 min

Ingredients:

1 lb ground beef

1 onion, grated

1 egg, lightly whisked

1 tbsp dried parsley

1 tsp garlic powder

1 tsp dried basil

1 tsp dried oregano

1/4 cup olive oil

Directions:

Combine ground beef, onion, egg, parsley, garlic powder, basil and oregano. Mix very well with hands. Roll tablespoonfuls of the meat mixture into balls.

Place meatballs on a lined baking tray. Bake 20 minutes or until brown. Transfer to a serving plate and serve.

Marinated Beef Skewers

Serves 4

Prep time: 30 min

Ingredients:

2 lbs beef, cut into 1 inch cubes

2 small onions, quartered

2 cups small mushrooms, whole

2 red bell peppers, cut

for the marinade:

2 tbsp lemon juice

1/4 cup olive oil

2 garlic cloves, crushed

1 tsp dried oregano

1 tbsp Dijon mustard

Directions:

Prepare the marinade by mixing all ingredients until smooth.

Cut the beef and place it in a bowl then pour over the marinade and set aside in a refrigerator for at least an hour.

Thread beef cubes onto skewers, dividing the cubes with mushrooms, peppers and onions.

Preheat BBQ grill to medium heat. Grill the beef skewers for about 2-3 minutes each side for medium cooked.

Mediterranean Steak

Serves 4

Prep time: 20 min

Ingredients:

4 sirloin steaks, trimmed

6 large tomatoes, sliced

1 onion, sliced

2 tsp baby capers

1 tbsp dried basil

3 garlic cloves, crushed

1 tbsp lemon juice

1/4 cup extra virgin olive oil

salt and black pepper, to taste

Directions:

Place steaks in a shallow dish. Rub both sides with half the olive oil, garlic, herbs, and black pepper. Set aside in a refrigerator for 1 hour.

Preheat oven to 350 F. Arrange tomatoes on a baking tray lined with baking paper. Scatter over capers and onion slices. Sprinkle with the remaining olive oil and cook for 15 minutes.

Heat a non-stick grill pan over high heat. Cook steaks to desired doneness, 4 minutes per side for rare.

Serve on a bed of roasted tomatoes and onions.

Italian Pot Roast

Serves 6

Prep time: 120 min

Ingredients:

4 garlic cloves, crushed

2 onions, sliced

6 carrots, quartered

4 celery ribs, cut into thick pieces

2 bay leaves

1 tbsp finely chopped rosemary

1/4 tsp black pepper

1 tbsp dried basil

1 tbsp dried oregano

1/4 cup olive oil

Directions:

Combine all the spice in a small bowl. Heat the olive oil in a large oven-proof dish and immediately seal all sides of the roast. Coat it with the spice mix.

Put roast in the middle of the baking dish. Crush the garlic and add it to the dish together with the onions, bay leaves, carrots and celery.

Cover and bake at 325 degrees 1 1/2 -2 hours, or until cooked to your liking.

Roast Beef with Quince, Parsnips and Carrots

Serves 6

Prep time: 60-70 min

Ingredients:

2-3 lb roast beef round

4 parsnips, peeled, quartered lengthwise

6 carrots, quartered lengthwise

2 quinces, peeled, cored and cubed

1 cup beef or chicken broth

2 tbsp apple puree

1 tbsp Dijon mustard

3 tbsp extra virgin olive oil

black pepper, to taste

Directions:

Whisk together beef broth, apple puree and mustard until smooth.

Heat the olive oil in a large frying pan over high heat and seal all sides of the roast. Transfer roast to a baking dish.

Arrange the parsnips around the beef. Sprinkle with black pepper and roast for 15 minutes. Add in the carrots and roast, stirring the vegetables once, for a further 25 minutes. Add in the quince. Brush the beef with the apple puree and mustard mixture.

Cover and bake at 325 degrees 30 minutes, or until cooked to your liking.

Eggplant With Ground Beef

Serves: 6

Prep time: 45 min

Ingredients:

1 lb ground beef

2 eggplants, peeled and cut into thick rounds

1 tbsp salt

1 onion, chopped

2 garlic cloves, crushed

1/2 tsp ground cinnamon

1/2 tsp ground nutmeg

1/4 tsp ground coriander

1 can tomatoes, undrained, chopped

1/2 cup parsley leaves, finely chopped

2 eggs

3 tbsp milk

4 tbsp extra virgin olive oil

salt and black pepper, to taste

Directions:

Peel and cut the eggplant and place the slices on a plate. Sprinkle with a tablespoon of salt and set aside for 30 minutes, then rinse and pat dry.

Heat olive oil in a deep frying pan over medium-high heat. Fry the eggplant slices in batches for 2-3 minutes each side or until golden. Set aside in a plate.

In the same pan, sauté onion and garlic for 2-3 minutes or until transparent. Add in ground beef and spice, mix well and sauté until it turns light brown. Add in tomatoes and parsley and simmer until the tomato sauce thickens.

Place half the eggplant slices in an ovenproof baking dish. Cover with beef and tomato mixture and top with remaining eggplant.

Whisk two eggs with milk. Pour over the meat and eggplant mixture. Bake for 30 minutes or until golden. Set aside for five minutes and serve.

Steak with Olives and Mushrooms

Serves: 6

Prep time: 20 min

Ingredients:

1 lb boneless beef sirloin steak, 3/4-inch thick, cut into 4 pieces

1 large onion, sliced

5-6 white mushrooms

1/2 cup green olives, coarsely chopped

4 tbsp extra virgin olive oil

1 cup parsley leaves, finely cut

Directions:

Heat olive oil in a heavy bottomed skillet over medium-high heat. Cook the steaks until well browned on both sides then set aside in a plate.

Gently sauté the onion in the same skillet, for 2-3 minutes, stirring occasionally. Add in the mushrooms and olives and cook until the mushrooms are done.

Return the steaks to the skillet, cover, and cook for 5-6 minutes. Stir in parsley and serve.

Mediterranean Beef Casserole

Serves: 5-6

Prep time: 80 min

Ingredients:

2 lbs boneless lean beef stew meat, cut into 1 1/2-inch cubes

1 onion, sliced

2 garlic cloves, chopped

2 carrots, cut

1 fennel bulb, trimmed and thinly sliced vertically

1 zucchini, cut

3 tomatoes, quartered

2 tbsp tomato paste

1/2 cup black olives, pitted

1/2 cup chicken broth

2 tbsp extra virgin olive oil

1 bay leaf

1 tsp dried basil

salt and black pepper, to taste

Directions:

Heat the olive oil in a deep saucepan and brown the beef. Dilute the tomato paste in the broth and pour over the beef mixture. Add in the olives, bay leaf and basil and simmer, covered, for 60 minutes.

Add all vegetables and simmer for 20 minutes more.

Beef with Melting Onions

Serves: 6

Prep time: 120 min

Ingredients:

2 lb stewing beef

4 large onions, sliced

3 garlic cloves, chopped

1 bay leaf

1/2 cup chicken broth

4 tbsp extra virgin olive oil

1 tsp cinnamon

1/2 tsp ginger powder

salt and black pepper, to taste

Directions:

Heat olive oil in a large saucepan and brown the beef. Add in onions and garlic and sauté for 2-3 minutes, stirring. Add cinnamon, ginger, bay leaf, black pepper and chicken broth.

Bring to a boil. Reduce heat to low, cover, and simmer for 2 hours, stirring occasionally, until the beef is tender.

Beef with Mushrooms

Serves: 4-5

Prep time: 90 min

Ingredients:

2 lb stewing beef

2 lb white mushrooms, sliced

1 onion, finely cut

6 tbsp extra virgin olive oil

1/2 cup white wine

1 tsp dried thyme

1 tsp salt

1/2 cup fresh parsley, finely cut

black pepper, to taste

Directions:

Gently heat olive oil in a deep saucepan and cook the beef until well browned. Add in onion and sauté for 1-2 minutes until fragrant. Add in thyme and black pepper and stir to combine.

Add the mushrooms and the white wine, cover, and simmer, stirring from time to time, for 90 minutes or until the beef is cooked through.

Beef and Spinach Stew

Serves: 4-5

Prep time: 90 min

Ingredients:

2 lb stewing beef

1 bag frozen spinach

1 onion, finely cut

2 garlic cloves, pressed

1/2 cup chicken broth

1 tomato, chopped

4 tbsp extra virgin olive oil

salt and pepper, to taste

Directions:

In a deep saucepan, heat olive oil and brown the beef. Add in onion and garlic and sauté until just fragrant.

Add chicken broth and bring to a boil then reduce heat and simmer, covered, for 80 minutes. Add in spinach and tomato, stir and simmer for 10 more minutes.

Spring Beef Stew

Serves: 4-5

Prep time: 90 min

Ingredients:

2 lbs stewing beef

5 white mushrooms, chopped

3 bunches spring onions, finely cut

2 tomatoes, chopped

3 tbsp olive oil

1 tsp paprika

1 cup fresh mint, finely cut

2 cups fresh parsley, finely cut

Directions:

Heat olive oil in a deep skillet. Sauté lamb pieces until browned. Add onions and cook some more. Add paprika, cover and cook for an hour or until tender.

Add spring onions, mushrooms, tomatoes, mint and parsley and simmer for 10-15 more minutes.

Uncover and cook for a few more minutes, until the liquid evaporates.

Beef Tagine with Sweet Potatoes

Serves: 4-5

Prep time: 120 min

Ingredients:

2 lbs stewing beef

½ tsp turmeric

½ tsp black pepper

4-5 tbsp olive oil

1/2 tsp paprika

1/4 tsp ground ginger

½ tsp cumin

1 onion, finely chopped

1 bunch of fresh cilantro

1 bunch of fresh parsley

2 ripe tomatoes, peeled and sliced

1 lb sweet potatoes, peeled and cut into slices

Directions:

In an deep casserole dish, heat olive oil and sauté the beef until well browned. Add in onion, turmeric, salt, black pepper and all remaining spices.

Tie the parsley and cilantro together into a bouquet and place on top of the beef.

Cover, bring to a boil, immediately reduce heat, and simmer for 60 minutes until the meat is tender.

Remove from heat, remove the parsley and cilantro bouquet and add the sweet potatoes on top of the beef. Place the tomatoes on top of the sweet potatoes.

Cover again and simmer for 40 minutes, until the meat and potatoes are tender.

Stuffed Bell Peppers

Serves: 4-5

Prep time: 40 min

Ingredients:

1 lb lean ground beef

5-6 red bell peppers

1 onion, grated

2 garlic cloves, chopped

1 tomato, diced

1/3 cup pine nuts, toasted

5 tbsp extra virgin olive oil

1/2 cup finely cut parsley

1/3 cup water

1 tbsp paprika

salt and pepper, to taste

Directions:

Heat olive oil in a skillet pot and gently sauté onions and garlic until transparent. Add in ground beef, paprika, tomato, parsley, and pine nuts. Cook for 2-3 minutes, stirring. Season with salt and pepper and remove from heat.

Spoon beef mixture into peppers. Arrange the stuffed peppers in a deep pot in one layer. Add in water and bing to a boil.

Reduce heat and simmer for about 30 minutes.

Ground Beef and Cabbage Casserole

Serves: 4-5

Prep time: 50 min

Ingredients:

1 lb ground beef

1/2 cabbage, shredded

1/2 onion, chopped

2 leeks, white part only, chopped

1 tomato, diced

1 tbsp paprika

1/2 tsp cumin

½ tsp black pepper

4 tbsp extra virgin olive oil

salt, to taste

Directions:

In a deep saucepan, sauté the onion and leeks in olive oil until tender. Add in the ground beef, tomato, paprika, cumin, salt and black pepper.

Place shredded cabbage on the bottom of an ovenproof baking dish. Cover with beef mixture.

Cover with a lid or aluminum foil and bake at 325 F for 40 minutes.

Ground Beef and Lentil Casserole

Serves: 4-5

Prep time: 30 min

Ingredients:

1 lb ground beef

1 small onion, chopped

2 garlic cloves, crushed

1 cup dry green lentils

1 carrot, chopped

2 cups water

2 bay leaves

1 tsp dried oregano

1 tbsp paprika

1/2 tsp salt

1/2 tsp cumin

3 tbsp extra virgin olive oil

black pepper, to taste

Directions:

Heat the olive oil in a casserole over medium-high heat. Add the onion and carrot and sauté for 4-5 minutes. Add in garlic and sauté a minute more.

Add the ground beef and cook for 4-5 minutes, stirring, until browned. Add the paprika, cumin, oregano, bay leaves, tomatoes, lentils and water.

Bring everything to a boil then reduce heat and simmer for 20 minutes, or until the beef is cooked through. Remove the bay leaves and serve.

Salmon Kebabs

Serves: 4-5

Prep time: 30 min

Ingredients:

2 shallots, ends trimmed, halved

2 zucchinis, cut in 2 inch cubes

1 cup cherry tomatoes

6 skinless salmon fillets, cut into 1 inch pieces

3 limes, cut into thin wedges

Directions:

Preheat barbecue or char grill on medium-high. Thread fish cubes onto skewers, then zucchinis, shallots and tomatoes. Repeat to make 12 kebabs.

Bake the kebabs for about 3 minutes each side for medium cooked.

Transfer to a plate, cover with foil and set aside for 5 minutes to rest.

Mediterranean Baked Salmon

Serves: 4-5

Prep time: 35 min

Ingredients:

2 (6 oz) boneless salmon fillets

1 tomato, thinly sliced

1 onion, thinly sliced

1 tbsp capers

3 tbsp olive oil

1 tsp dry oregano

3 tbsp Parmesan cheese

salt and black pepper, to taste

Directions:

Preheat oven to 350 F. Place the salmon fillets in a baking dish, sprinkle with oregano, top with onion and tomato slices, drizzle with olive oil, and sprinkle with capers and Parmesan cheese.

Cover the dish with foil and bake for 30 minutes, or until the fish flakes easily.

Simple Oven-Baked Sea Bass

Serves: 4

Prep time: 35 min

Ingredients:

1 lb sea bass (cleaned and scaled

5 oz fennel, trimmed and sliced

5-6 spring onions, chopped

2 garlic cloves, chopped

10 black olives, pitted and halved

2-3 lemon wedges

1 tbsp capers

2 garlic cloves, finely chopped

½ tsp paprika

½ cup dry white wine

3 tbsp extra virgin olive oil

salt and pepper, to taste

Directions:

In a cup, mix garlic, olive oil, salt, and black pepper.

Arrange the sliced fennel in a shallow ovenproof casserole. Add the green onions and lay the fish on top. Pour over the olive mixture. Scatter the olives, paprika and lemon wedges over the fish, then pour the wine over the top.

Cover the dish with a lid or foil and bake for 30 minutes, or until the fish flakes easily.

Feta Cheese Baked in Foil

Serves: 4

Prep time: 15 min

Ingredients:

14 oz feta cheese, cut in slices

4 oz butter

1 tbsp paprika

1 tsp dried oregano

aluminum foil, enough to cover 4 slices of cheese

Directions:

Cut the cheese into four medium-thick slices and place on sheets of butter lined aluminum foil.

Place a little bit of butter on top each feta cheese piece, sprinkle with paprika and dried oregano and wrap. Place on a tray and bake in a preheated to 350 F oven for 15 minutes.

Creamy Avocado Spaghetti

Serves: 5-6

Prep time: 20 min

Ingredients:

12 oz spaghetti

1/2 cup black olives, halved

1 red pepper, cut in thin strips

2 avocados, peeled and diced

1 cup cherry tomatoes, halved

2 cloves garlic, finely chopped

1 tbsp basil pesto

5 tbsp extra virgin olive oil

4 tbsp lemon juice

1/4 cup grated Parmesan cheese

Directions:

In a large pot of boiling salted water, cook spaghetti according to package instructions. Drain and set aside in a large bowl.

In a blender, combine lemon juice, garlic, basil pesto and avocados and blend until smooth.

Combine spaghetti, olives, cherry tomatoes, pepper and avocado sauce. Sprinkle with Parmesan cheese and serve immediately.

Avocado, Roasted Mushroom and Feta Spaghetti

Serves: 5-6

Prep time: 20 min

Ingredients:

12 oz spaghetti

2 avocados, peeled and diced

10-15 white mushrooms, halved

1 cup feta, crumbled

2 tbsp green olive paste

2 garlic cloves, chopped

olive oil spay

salt and black pepper, to taste

Directions:

Line a baking tray with baking paper and place mushrooms on it. Spray with olive oil and season with salt and black pepper to taste. Roast in a preheated to 375 F oven for 15 minutes, or until golden and tender.

In a large pot of boiling salted water, cook spaghetti according to package instructions. Drain and set aside in a large bowl.

In a blender, combine lemon juice, garlic, olive paste and avocados and blend until smooth.

Combine pasta, mushrooms and avocado sauce. Sprinkle with feta cheese and serve immediately.

Tomato, Arugula and Feta Spaghetti

Serves: 5-6

Prep time: 20 min

Ingredients:

12 oz spaghetti

2 cups grape tomatoes, halved

1 cup fresh basil leaves, roughly torn

1 cup baby arugula leaves

1 cup feta, crumbled

2 garlic cloves, chopped

5 tbsp extra virgin olive oil

salt and black pepper, to taste

Directions:

In a large saucepan of boiling salted water, cook spaghetti according to package instructions. Drain and set aside in a large bowl.

Return saucepan to medium heat. Add olive oil, garlic and tomatoes. Season with pepper and cook, tossing, for 1-2 minutes or until tomatoes are hot. Add spaghetti, basil and feta. Toss gently for 1 minute or until heated through. Sprinkle with arugula and serve.

Mediterranean Pizza

Serves: 4

Prep time: 35 min

Ingredients:

1 store-bought or homemade dough

3-4 green onions, chopped

1 (6 oz) can quartered artichoke hearts, drained

1/2 cup red bell pepper, chopped

1 garlic clove, chopped

1 cup black olives, chopped

1 cup baby arugula leaves

1/2 cup fresh tomato sauce

1 cup (4 oz) crumbled goat cheese

3 tbsp extra virgin olive oil

1 tbsp dried basil

salt and black pepper, to taste

Directions:

Heat a large skillet on medium heat and sauté the onion and bell pepper for 2-3 minutes until fragrant. Add in the artichoke hearts, garlic, olives and basil and sauté for 5 minutes more. Season with salt and black pepper to taste.

Roll out dough onto a floured surface and transfer to a parchment-lined 12 inch round baking sheet.

Top it with tomato sauce, goat cheese and the sautéed vegetables.

Bake for 30 minutes in a preheated to 450 F oven or until the crust is golden brown and the sauce is bubbly. Set aside for 5 minutes, cut, and serve.

Delicious One-Pot Pasta

Serves: 4-5

Prep time: 35 min

Ingredients:

12 oz dry pasta

1/2 onion, chopped

1 small eggplant, peeled and cubed

1 small zucchini, peeled and cubed

2-3 garlic cloves, crushed

2/3 cup canned chickpeas drained

1.5 cups marinara sauce

2 cups water

3 tbsp extra virgin olive oil

1 cup grated Parmesan cheese

1/2 cup fresh parsley, finely cut

1 tsp salt

1 tsp fresh black pepper

Directions:

Heat a deep saucepan over medium-high heat. Add in olive oil and gently sauté the onion, eggplant, garlic, chickpeas, and zucchini. Stir in pasta, water, and marinara sauce.

Season with salt and black pepper, bring to a boil, cover, and simmer until the pasta is cooked to al dente. Sprinkle with parsley, Parmesan cheese, and serve.

Easy One-Pot Spaghetti

Serves: 4-5

Ingredients:

12 oz spaghetti

1/2 onion, chopped

1 lb boneless chicken breast half, cooked and diced

1 (6 oz) can artichoke hearts, drained

1/2 can chickpeas, drained

2 garlic cloves, crushed

1.5 cups tomato sauce

2 cups water

3 tbsp extra virgin olive oil

1 tsp dried basil

1 tsp dried oregano

1/3 cup fresh parsley, finely cut

1/3 cup crumbled feta cheese

Directions:

Heat a large saucepan over medium-high heat. Add in olive oil and gently sauté the onion, garlic, chicken, chickpeas, artichoke hearts, water, and tomato sauce. Season with salt and black pepper and bring to a boil.

Add in spaghetti, basil and oregano, and stir. Reduce heat and simmer until the spaghetti is cooked to al dente.

Sprinkle with parsley and feta cheese, and serve.

Hearty Lentil Spaghetti

Serves: 4-5

Prep time: 35 min

Ingredients:

12 oz spaghetti

1/2 onion, chopped

1 can brown lentils, rinsed, drained

1 cup green olives, pitted and halved

1-2 garlic cloves, chopped

2 cups tomato sauce

2 cups water

3 tbsp extra virgin olive oil

1/3 cup fresh mint, finely cut

1 tsp salt

1 cup crumbled feta cheese

Directions:

Heat a deep saucepan over medium-high heat. Add in olive oil and gently sauté the onion, garlic, lentils, olives, water and tomato sauce.

Bring to a boil, then add spaghetti and stir. Reduce heat and simmer until the spaghetti is cooked to al dente.

Sprinkle with feta cheese and mint, adjust seasonings, and serve.

Ratatouille

Serves: 4

Prep time: 45 min

Ingredients:

1 eggplant, peeled and diced

2 large tomatoes, diced

2 zucchinis, peeled and sliced

1 onion, sliced

1 green pepper, sliced

6-7 mushrooms, sliced

3 cloves garlic, crushed

1 tbsp dried parsley

½ cup Parmesan cheese

3 tbsp extra virgin olive oil

salt, to taste

Directions:

Place eggplant on a tray and sprinkle with salt. Set aside for 30 minutes, then rinse and pat dry.

Heat olive oil in an ovenproof casserole dish over medium heat. Gently sauté garlic until fragrant. Add in parsley and eggplant and cook until eggplant is soft. Sprinkle with a tablespoon of Parmesan cheese.

Spread zucchinis in an even layer over the eggplant. Sprinkle with cheese again.

Layer onion, mushrooms, pepper and tomatoes, covering each

layer with a sprinkling of Parmesan cheese.

Bake in a preheated to 350 F oven for 40 minutes.

Spicy Chickpea and Spinach Stew

Serves: 4

Prep time: 40 min

Ingredients:

1 onion, chopped

3 garlic cloves, chopped

1 15 oz can chickpeas, drained and rinsed

1 15 oz can tomatoes, diced and undrained

1 1 lb bag baby spinach

a handful of blanched almonds

½ cup vegetable broth

1 tbsp hot chilli paste

½ tsp cumin

salt and pepper, to taste

Directions:

Heat olive oil in a large saucepan over medium-high heat. Gently sauté onion and garlic for 4-5 minutes, or until tender. Add spices and stir.

Add in chickpeas, tomatoes, almonds and broth. Bring to a boil, then reduce heat to low and simmer, partially covered, for 10 minutes.

Add the chilli paste and spinach to the pot and stir until the spinach wilts. Remove from heat and season with salt and pepper to taste.

Moroccan Chickpea Stew

Serves: 4-5

Prep time: 20 min

Ingredients:

1 onion, chopped

3 garlic cloves, chopped

2 large carrots, chopped

2 potatoes, peeled and chopped

4-5 dates, pitted and chopped

1 cup spinach, chopped

1 15 oz can tomatoes, diced and undrained

1 15 oz can chickpeas, rinsed and drained

1 cup vegetable broth

1 tbsp ground cumin

½ tsp chilli powder

½ tsp ground turmeric

½ teaspoon salt

3 tbsp extra virgin olive oil

½ cup chopped cilantro, to serve

grated lemon zest, to serve

Directions:

Heat olive oil in a large saucepan over medium-high heat. Gently sauté onion, garlic and carrots for 4-5 minutes, or until tender. Add all spices and stir. Stir in all other ingredients except the spinach.

Bring to a boil, cover, reduce heat, and simmer for 20 minutes, or until potatoes are tender.

Add in spinach, stir and cook it until it wilts. Serve over brown rice, quinoa or couscous and top with chopped cilantro and lemon zest.

Zucchini Fritters

Serves: 4

Prep time: 20 min

Ingredients:

5 zucchinis, grated

3 eggs

2 garlic cloves, crushed

5 spring onions, finely chopped

1 cup feta cheese, crumbled

1/2 cup fresh dill, finely cut

salt and black pepper, to taste

1 cup flour

1 cup sunflower oil

Directions:

Grate zucchinis and put them in a colander. Sprinkle with salt and leave aside to drain. After 20 minutes, squeeze and place in a bowl.

Add in all other ingredients except for the flour and sunflower oil. Combine everything very well. Add in flour and stir to combine again.

Heat the sunflower oil in a frying pan. Drop a few scoops of the zucchini batter and fry them on medium heat for 3-5 minutes, until golden brown. Serve with yogurt.

Baked Falafel

Serves: 7

Prep time: 20-30 min

Ingredients:

1 can chickpeas, drained and rinsed

1 small carrot, cut

1 onion, cut

2 garlic cloves, minced

½ cup fresh parsley, finely cut

¼ cup whole wheat flour

¼ cup tahini

1/4 cup extra virgin olive oil

2-3 tbsp lemon juice

2 tsp cumin (or to taste)

1 tsp salt

black pepper, to taste

Directions:

Blend the carrots, chickpeas, onion and garlic in a food processor until completely minced. When it turns to a smooth paste, add in parsley and transfer to a large mixing bowl. Stir in the remaining ingredients.

Using a large tablespoon form batter into burgers. Bake in a preheated to 375F oven until golden.

Chickpea, Rice and Mushroom Stew

Serves: 4-5

Prep time: 20-30 min

Ingredients:

1 15 oz can chickpeas, drained

1 large onion, finely cut

2 cups mushrooms, chopped

2 carrots, chopped

1 15 oz can tomatoes, diced, undrained

1/3 cup rice, washed

1 cup vegetable broth

4 tbsp extra virgin olive oil

1 tsp oregano

1 tbsp paprika

1 cup fresh parsley, finely cut

1 tbsp sugar

Directions:

In a deep, heavy-bottomed saucepan, heat olive oil and gently sauté the onion and carrots for 4-5 minutes, stirring constantly. Add in paprika, chickpeas, rice, mushrooms, tomatoes, sugar and vegetable broth and stir again.

Season with salt, oregano, ground black pepper and bring to the boil. Cover, reduce heat, and simmer for about 20 minutes, stirring from time to time.

Sprinkle with parsley, simmer for a minute more and serve.

Chickpea, Leek and Olive Stew

Serves: 4-5

Prep time: 20 min

Ingredients:

5 cups sliced leeks

25-30 black olives, pitted and halved

1 15 oz can chickpeas, drained

½ cup water

1 tbsp tomato paste

1 cup grated Parmesan cheese

4 tbsp extra virgin olive oil

salt and black pepper, to taste

Directions:

In a deep baking dish, heat olive oil and sauté the leeks for 2-3 minutes. Add in the chickpeas and olives. Dissolve the tomato paste in half a cup of warm water and add it to the chickpeas.

Season with black pepper and bake in a preheated to 350 F oven for 15-20 minutes.

Sprinkle with Parmesan cheese and bake for 3-4 minutes more. Serve and enjoy!

Baked Bean and Rice Casserole

Serves: 4-5

Prep time: 30 min

Ingredients:

2 15 oz cans white or red beans, drained

1 cup water or vegetable broth

2/3 cup rice

2 onions, chopped

1 cup parsley, finely cut

7-8 fresh mint leaves, finely cut

3 tbsp extra virgin olive oil

1 tbsp paprika

½ tsp black pepper

1 tsp salt

Directions:

Heat olive oil in an ovenproof casserole dish and gently sauté the chopped onions for 1-2 minutes. Stir in paprika and rice and cook, stirring constantly, for another minute.

Add in beans and a cup of water or vegetable broth, season with salt and black pepper, stir in mint and parsley, and bake in a preheated to 350 F oven for 20 minutes.

Green Pea and Rice Casserole

Serves: 4-5

Prep time: 20 min

Ingredients:

1 onion, chopped

1 1 lb bag frozen peas

3 garlic cloves, chopped

3-4 mushrooms, chopped

2/3 cup white rice

1 cup water

2/3 cup grated Parmesan cheese

4 tbsp extra virgin olive oil

salt and black pepper, to taste

Directions:

In a deep ovenproof casserole dish, heat olive oil and sauté the onions, garlic and mushrooms for 2-3 minutes. Add in the rice and cook, stirring constantly for 1 minute.

Add in a cup of warm water and the frozen peas, stir and bake in a preheated to 350 F oven for 20 minutes. Sprinkle with Parmesan cheese, bake for 2-3 more minutes and serve.

Easy Green Bean Stew

Serves: 4-5

Prep time: 20 min

Ingredients:

2 10 oz bags frozen green beans

1 large onion, finely cut

2 carrots, sliced

1 tomato, diced

3-4 garlic cloves, chopped

1 cup fresh dill, finely chopped

1 tbsp chia seeds

4 tbsp extra virgin olive oil

1 tsp salt

1 tbsp paprika

Directions:

Heat olive oil in a deep casserole dish and gently sauté the onions and the garlic. Add in the paprika and carrots and stir. Add the green beans and the tomato.

Bring to the boil then lower heat and simmer, covered, for about 30 minutes. Sprinkle with chia seeds, fresh dill, and serve.

Green Beans and Potatoes

Serves: 4-4

Prep time: 20 min

Ingredients:

1 bag frozen green beans

3 potatoes, peeled and diced

1 tsp tomato paste

1 carrot, sliced

1 onion, chopped

2 garlic cloves, crushed

3 tbsp extra virgin olive oil

1/2 cup fresh dill, finely chopped

½ cup water

1 tsp paprika

salt and pepper, to taste

Directions:

Heat olive oil in a deep saucepan and sauté the onion for 2-3 minutes, stirring. Add in garlic and sauté until just fragrant. Add in the green beans, and all remaining ingredients.

Stir to combine very well, cover, and simmer for about 20-30 minutes until all vegetables are tender. Serve warm sprinkled with fresh dill.

Cabbage and Rice Stew

Serves: 4

Prep time: 25 min

Ingredients:

1 cup white rice

½ medium head cabbage, cored and shredded

1 small onion, chopped

2 tomatoes, diced

1 cup hot water

2 tbsp extra virgin olive oil

1 tbsp paprika

1 tsp cumin

salt, to taste

black pepper, to taste

Directions:

Heat olive oil in a large ovenproof baking dish and gently sauté onion until transparent. Add in paprika, cumin, rice and water, stir, and bring to a boil. Simmer for 5 minutes then add in the shredded cabbage and tomatoes.

Stir to combine well and bake in a preheated to 350 F oven for about 20 minutes, stirring occasionally. Season with salt and black pepper to taste, and set aside for 4-5 minutes.

Serve sprinkled with fresh parsley.

Baked Cauliflower

Serves: 4

Prep time: 25 min

Ingredients:

1 small cauliflower, cut into florets

1 tbsp garlic powder

1 tsp paprika

salt, to taste

black pepper, to taste

4 tbsp extra virgin olive oil

1/2 cup grated Parmesan cheese

Directions:

Combine olive oil, paprika, salt, pepper and garlic powder together. Toss in the cauliflower florets and place in a baking dish in one layer.

Bake in a preheated to 350 F oven for 20 minutes. Take out of the oven, stir, and sprinkle with Parmesan cheese. Bake for 5 minutes more or until golden.

Potato and Zucchini Bake

Serves: 5-6

Prep time: 25 min

Ingredients:

1 lb potatoes, peeled and sliced

4-5 zucchinis, peeled and sliced

1 onion, sliced

2 garlic cloves, crushed

½ cup water

4 tbsp extra virgin olive oil

1 tsp dry oregano

1/3 cup fresh dill, chopped

1 cup grated Parmesan cheese

salt and black pepper, to taste

Directions:

Place the potatoes, zucchinis and onion in a shallow ovenproof baking dish. Pour over the olive oil and water. Add salt, black pepper to taste, and toss everything together.

Bake in a preheated to 350 F oven for 40 minutes, stirring halfway through. sprinkle with dill and Parmesan cheese, bake for 5 minutes more and serve.

Okra and Tomato Casserole

Serves: 4

Prep time: 25 min

Ingredients:

1 lb okra, trimmed

3 tomatoes, cut into wedges

3 garlic cloves, chopped

1 cup fresh parsley leaves, finely cut

3 tbsp extra virgin olive oil

1 tsp salt

black pepper, to taste

Directions:

In a deep ovenproof baking dish, combine okra, sliced tomatoes, olive oil and garlic. Add in salt and black pepper to taste, and toss to combine.

Bake in a preheated to 350 F oven for 45 minutes, or until the okra is tender. Sprinkle with parsley and serve.

Breakfast and Dessert Recipes

Avocado and Feta Toast with Poached Eggs

Serves: 4

Prep time: 5 min

Ingredients:

1 avocado, peeled and chopped

½ cup feta cheese, crumbled

2 tbsp chopped fresh mint

1 tsp lime juice

½ tsp cumin

4 thick slices rye bread, lightly toasted

4 poached eggs

Directions:

Mash avocados with a fork until almost smooth. Add the feta, fresh mint, lime juice and cumin. Season with salt and pepper to taste. Stir to combine.

Toast 4 slices of rye bread until golden. Spoon 1/4 of the avocado mixture onto each slice of bread. Top with a poached egg and serve immediately.

Avocado and Olive Paste on Toasted Rye Bread

Serves: 4

Prep time: 5 min

Ingredients:

1 avocado, halved, peeled and finely chopped

1 tbsp green onions, finely chopped

2 tbsp green olive paste

4 lettuce leaves

1 tbsp lemon juice

Directions:

Mash avocados with a fork or potato masher until almost smooth. Add the onions, green olive paste and lemon juice. Season with salt and pepper to taste. Stir to combine.

Toast 4 slices of rye bread until golden. Spoon 1/4 of the avocado mixture onto each slice of bread, top with a lettuce leaf and serve.

Avocado and Chickpea Sandwiches

Serves: 4

Prep time: 3-4 min

Ingredients:

4 slices white bread

1/2 cup canned chickpeas

1 small avocado

2 green onions, finely chopped

1 egg, hard boiled

1/2 tomato, thinly sliced

1/2 cucumber, thinly sliced

salt, to taste

Directions:

Mash the avocado and chickpeas with a fork or potato masher until smooth. Add in green onions and salt and combine well.

Spread this mixture on the four slices of bread. Top each slice with tomato, cucumber and egg, and serve.

Quick Vegetable Omelette

Serves: 4

Prep time: 10 min

Ingredients:

1/2 small onion, chopped

2 tomatoes, diced

1/4 cup fresh peas

6 eggs

10 oz feta cheese, crumbled

4 tbsp extra virgin olive oil

black pepper, to taste

salt, to taste

Directions:

In a large pan sauté onion over medium heat for 1-2 minutes, stirring. Add in tomatoes and peas and simmer until the peas are soft and the mixture is almost dry.

Add in feta cheese and eggs, stir, and cook until well mixed and not too liquid.

Season with black pepper and serve.

Raisin Quinoa Breakfast

Serves: 4

Prep time: 15 min

Ingredients:

1 cup quinoa

2 cups milk

2 tbsp walnuts, crushed

2 tbsp raisins

2 tbsp dried cranberries

2-3 tbsp honey, optional

½ tsp vanilla extract

1 tbsp chia seeds

Directions:

Rinse quinoa with cold water and drain. Place milk and quinoa into a saucepan and bring to a boil. Add vanilla.

Reduce heat to low and simmer for about 15 minutes stirring from time to time.

Set aside to cool then serve in a bowl, topped with honey, chia seeds, raisins, cranberries and crushed walnuts.

Banana Cinnamon Fritters

Serves: 4

Prep time: 15 min

Ingredients:

1 cup self-raising flour

1 egg, beaten

3/4 cup sparkling water

2 tsp ground cinnamon

sunflower oil, for frying

2-3 bananas, cut diagonally into 4 pieces each

powdered sugar, to serve

Directions:

Sift flour and cinnamon into a bowl and make a well in the centre. Add egg and enough sparkling water to mix to a smooth batter.

Heat sunflower oil in a saucepan, enough to cover the base by 1-2 inch, so when a little batter dropped into the oil sizzles and rises to the surface.

Dip banana pieces into the batter, then fry for 2-3 minutes or until golden. Remove with a slotted spoon and drain on paper towels. Sprinkle with sugar and serve hot.

Avocado and Pumpkin Muffins

Serves: 13-14

Prep time: 20 min

Ingredients:

1/2 cup mashed avocado

1 1/2 cup pumpkin puree

2 large eggs

2 cups flour

1 cup sugar

1 tsp baking soda

1 tsp salt

1 tsp cinnamon

1 tsp vanilla extract

1/2 cup walnuts, coarsely chopped

Directions:

Preheat oven to 375 F. Grease a muffin tin or line with paper cups.

In a large bowl, mix avocado, pumpkin and eggs. In a separate bowl, whisk flour, sugar, baking soda, cinnamon, vanilla and salt. Combine with avocado mixture; do not over-mix. Stir in walnuts.

Spoon batter into prepared muffin tin; bake for 15-18 minutes or until tops start to brown and a toothpick inserted into a muffin comes out clean.

Moist Pear Muffins

Serves: 16

Prep time: 20 min

Ingredients:

2 1/2 cups flour

1 cup sugar

2 eggs

1 cup yogurt

1/2 cup milk

1/2 cup sunflower oil

2/3 cup small pear pieces, peeled

1 tsp baking soda

1 tsp vanilla extract

1 tsp lemon zest

Preheat oven to 375 F. Grease a muffin tin or line with paper cups.

Combine flour with sugar, chopped pear, vanilla and baking soda. Whisk eggs, yogurt, milk, lemon zest and sunflower oil in another bowl.

Pour wet mixture into dry mixture and stir until batter is just blended. Fill prepared muffin cups 3/4 full and bake for 20 minutes or until a toothpick comes out clean.

Set aside to cool in the pans for 10 minutes before removing on a wire rack.

Easy Lemon Cake

Serves: 12

Prep time: 20 min

Ingredients:

4 eggs

1/2 cup milk

1 cup sugar

1/2 cup sunflower oil

2 cups flour

1 tbsp baking powder

1/2 tsp salt

2 tbsp fresh lemon juice

2 tbsp lemon zest

1/2 tsp vanilla extract

Directions:

Whisk eggs and sugar until light and creamy. Gently add in the sunflower oil, flour, baking powder, salt, and milk. Beat until smooth, then add in lemon juice, lemon zest and vanilla.

Pour the batter into a prepared 10 inch tube pan and bake in a preheated to 350 F oven for about 40 minutes, or until a toothpick comes out clean.

Set aside to cool then turn onto a wire rack to finish cooling.

FREE BONUS RECIPES: 20 Superfood Paleo and Vegan Smoothies for Vibrant Health and Easy Weight Loss

Kale and Kiwi Smoothie

Serves: 2

Prep time: 2-3 min

Ingredients:

2-3 ice cubes

1 cup orange juice

1 small pear, peeled and chopped

2 kiwi, peeled and chopped

2-3 kale leaves

2-3 dates, pitted

Directions:

Combine all ingredients in a high speed blender and blend until smooth.

Delicious Broccoli Smoothie

Serves: 2

Prep time: 2-3 min

Ingredients:

2-3 frozen broccoli florets

1 cup coconut milk

1 banana, peeled and chopped

1 cup pineapple, cut

1 peach, chopped

1 tsp cinnamon

Directions:

Combine all ingredients in a high speed blender and blend until smooth.

Papaya Smoothie

Serves: 2

Prep time: 2-3 min

Ingredients:

2-3 frozen broccoli florets

1 cup orange juice

1 small ripe avocado, peeled, cored and diced

1 cup papaya

1 cup fresh strawberries

Directions:

Combine all ingredients in a high speed blender and blend until smooth.

Beet and Papaya Smoothie

Serves: 2

Prep time: 2-3 min

Ingredients:

3-4 ice cubes

1 cup orange juice

1 banana, peeled and chopped

1 cup papaya

1 small beet, peeled and cut

Directions:

Combine all ingredients in a high speed blender and blend until smooth.

Lean Green Smoothie

Serves: 2

Prep time: 2-3 min

Ingredients:

1 frozen banana, chopped

1 cup orange juice

2-3 kale leaves, stems removed

1 small cucumber, peeled and chopped

1/2 cup fresh parsley leaves

½ tsp grated ginger

Directions:

Combine all ingredients in a high speed blender and blend until smooth.

Easy Antioxidant Smoothie

Serves: 2

Prep time: 2-3 min

Ingredients:

2-3 frozen broccoli florets

1 cup orange juice

2 plums, cut

1 cup raspberries

1 tsp ginger powder

Directions:

Combine all ingredients in a high speed blender and blend until smooth.

Healthy Purple Smoothie

Serves: 2

Prep time: 2-3 min

Ingredients:

2-3 frozen broccoli florets

1 cup water

1/2 avocado, peeled and chopped

3 plums, chopped

1 cup blueberries

Directions:

Combine all ingredients in a high speed blender and blend until smooth.

Mom's Favorite Kale Smoothie

Serves: 2

Prep time: 2-3 min

Ingredients:

2-3 ice cubes

1½ cup orange juice

1 green small apple, cut

½ cucumber, chopped

2-3 leaves kale

½ cup raspberries

Directions:

Combine all ingredients in a high speed blender and blend until smooth.

Creamy Green Smoothie

Serves: 2

Prep time: 2-3 min

Ingredients:

1 frozen banana

1 cup coconut milk

1 small pear, chopped

1 cup baby spinach

1 cup grapes

1 tbsp coconut butter

1 tsp vanilla extract

Directions:

Combine all ingredients in a high speed blender and blend until smooth.

Strawberry and Arugula Smoothie

Serves: 2

Prep time: 2-3 min

Ingredients:

2 cups frozen strawberries

1 cup unsweetened almond milk

10-12 arugula leaves

1/2 tsp ground cinnamon

Directions:

Combine ice, almond milk, strawberries, arugula and cinnamon in a high speed blender. Blend until smooth and serve.

Emma's Amazing Smoothie

Serves: 2

Prep time: 2-3 min

Ingredients:

1 frozen banana, chopped

1 cup orange juice

1 large nectarine, sliced

1/2 zucchini, peeled and chopped

2-3 dates, pitted

Directions:

Combine all ingredients in a high speed blender and blend until smooth.

Good-To-Go Morning Smoothie

Serves: 2

Prep time: 2-3 min

Ingredients:

1 cup frozen strawberries

1 cup apple juice

1 banana, chopped

1 cup raw asparagus, chopped

1 tbsp ground flaxseed

Directions:

Combine all ingredients in a high speed blender and blend until smooth.

Endless Energy Smoothie

Serves: 2

Prep time: 2-3 min

Ingredients:

1 frozen banana, chopped

1 1/2 cup green tea

1 cup chopped pineapple

2 raw asparagus spears, chopped

1 lime, juiced

1 tbsp chia seeds

Directions:

Combine all ingredients in a high speed blender and blend until smooth.

High-fibre Fruit Smoothie

Serves: 2

Prep time: 2-3 min

Ingredients:

1 frozen banana, chopped

1 cup orange juice

2 cups chopped papaya

1 cup shredded cabbage

1 tbsp chia seeds

Directions:

Combine all ingredients in a high speed blender and blend until smooth.

Nutritious Green Smoothie

Serves: 2

Prep time: 2-3 min

Ingredients:

2-3 frozen broccoli florets

1 cup apple juice

1 large pear, chopped

1 kiwi, peeled and chopped

1 cup spinach leaves

1-2 dates, pitted

Directions:

Combine all ingredients in a high speed blender and blend until smooth.

Apricot, Strawberry and Banana Smoothie

Serves: 2

Prep time: 2-3 min

Ingredients:

1 frozen banana

1 1/2 cup almond milk

5 dried apricots

1 cup fresh strawberries

Directions:

Combine all ingredients in a high speed blender and blend until smooth.

Spinach and Green Apple Smoothie

Serves: 2

Prep time: 2-3 min

Ingredients:

3-4 ice cubes

1 cup unsweetened almond milk

1 banana, peeled and chopped

2 green apples, peeled and chopped

1 cup raw spinach leaves

3-4 dates, pitted

1 tsp grated ginger

Directions:

Combine all ingredients in a high speed blender and blend until smooth.

Superfood Blueberry Smoothie

Serves: 2

Prep time: 2-3 min

Ingredients:

2-3 cubes frozen spinach

1 cup green tea

1 banana

2 cups blueberries

1 tbsp ground flaxseed

Directions:

Combine all ingredients in a high speed blender and blend until smooth.

Zucchini and Blueberry Smoothie

Serves: 2

Prep time: 2-3 min

Ingredients:

1 cup frozen blueberries

1 cup unsweetened almond milk

1 banana

1 zucchini, peeled and chopped

Directions:

Combine all ingredients in a high speed blender and blend until smooth.

Tropical Spinach Smoothie

Serves: 2

Prep time: 2-3 min

Ingredients:

1/2 cup crushed ice or 3-4 ice cubes

1 cup coconut milk

1 mango, peeled and diced

1 cup fresh spinach leaves

4-5 dates, pitted

1/2 tsp vanilla extract

Directions:

Combine all ingredients in a high speed blender and blend until smooth.

About the Author

Alissa Grey is a fitness and nutrition enthusiast who loves to teach people about losing weight and feeling better about themselves. She lives in a small French village in the foothills of a beautiful mountain range with her husband, three teenage kids, two free spirited dogs, and various other animals.

Alissa is incredibly lucky to be able to cook and eat natural foods, mostly grown nearby, something she's done since she was a teenager. She enjoys yoga, running, reading, hanging out with her family, and growing organic vegetables and herbs.

Printed in Great Britain
by Amazon